PIVOT POINTS
Attitudes, Motivations, and Priorities
That Make a Difference

A RESEARCH REPORT

PUBLISHED by PARABLES
Earthly Stories with a Heavenly Meaning

A Note to the Reader:

While we reflected upon the information learned from this study, an acronym was identified that helped us remember the points. You will see the letters of the acronym highlighted at the beginning of each chapter listing in the Table of Contents. The acronym is:

GIVE X TAKE

A RESEARCH REPORT

PIVOT POINTS
Attitudes, Motivations, and Priorities
That Make a Difference

Dr. Steve R. Parr and Dr. Thomas Crites

Georgia Baptist
Mission Board

Gifts of Georgia Baptists through the Cooperative Program enable us to partner together in fulfilling the Great Commission

Copyright@2017 by The Georgia Baptist Mission Board
6405 Sugarloaf Parkway, Duluth, GA 30097

All rights reserved. No part of this publication may be reproduced in any form, except for brief quotations in reviews, without permission from the publisher.
ISBN: 978-1-945698-32-3
Printed in the United States
Published By Parables
504-715-1479

This project is dedicated to all pastors, staff ministers, and the associational missionaries of Georgia. We thank God for those who minister to the people of our communities with a commitment to the Lord Jesus Christ day in and day out. Our prayer is that the Lord may use this project to encourage you and to equip you to reach more for Jesus!

PUBLISHED by PARABLES
Earthly Stories with a Heavenly Meaning

ALSO BY DR. STEVE R. PARR

Key Strategies for a Healthy Sunday School
Sunday School That Really Works
Sunday School That Really Responds
Sunday School That Really Excels
The Coffee Shop That Changed a Church

CO-WRITTEN BY
DR. STEVE R. PARR & DR. TOM CRITES

Evangelistic Effectiveness:
Difference Makers in Mindsets and Methods
Why They Stay:
Helping Parents and Church Leaders
Make Investments that Keep Children and Teens
Connected to the Church for a Lifetime

CONTENTS

Foreword		11
Introduction		13

GIVE GENEROUSLY

Chapter One	**G**enerosity	21
Chapter Two	**I**ntentionality	33
Chapter Three	**V**itality	41
Chapter Four	**E**mpowering Members	49
Chapter Five	e**X**ceptional Leadership	59

TAKE INITIATIVE

Chapter Six	**T**ackling Priorities	69
Chapter Seven	**A**pproachability	75
Chapter Eight	**K**indness and Compassion	81
Chapter Nine	**E**xternal Connections	87
Appendix	Research Summary	93
Notes		98

ACKNOWLEDGMENTS

Thanks to Gary Bulley who endured hours of brainstorming and conversation regarding the genesis of this idea. Thanks to Andy Childs for his wisdom in the development of this project. Special thanks to Kathleen Harris, Bryan Nowak, Alicia Simpson, and Kevin Wilson for their expertise in working out the logistics for the survey. Thanks to Greg Abercrombie, Lex Bowen, Ray and Glynis Coleman, Steve Laughlin, JoJo Thomas, Harris Malcom, Charles Drummond, and Mike Everson for their input and contributions in the development of the study. Special thanks to John Dee Jeffries, Mark Strange, Eddy Oliver, and Elizabeth Locke for their assistance in the publication of this project.

FOREWORD

These are remarkable days as we see the evolution of technology that assist us in our everyday experiences. One of these is the Global Positioning System that allows us to use small devices as we drive, fly, or walk to accurately reach our destination. However, I was reminded recently that as a driver, I have the ultimate responsibility to get to my destination. While very reliable, the GPS systems we depend on are not infallible. We all know very well the voice of the little lady who lives in our cellphones and in various guidance devices. We have learned that sometimes she sends us in directions we don't want to go. Recently, she guided me in circles through a neighborhood that was irrelevant to the direction I needed to go. So, I finally broke away from her circuitous guidance to head in the defined direction. At that point, her personality was revealed as with an attitude she said, "Recalculating." I knew she was upset with me; since at least for that moment, I lost confidence in her guidance.

Because of these modern systems, the roadmap is often neglected, but I want to suggest to you that roadmaps still have great value. You cannot detect that you are being sent in the wrong direction, if you don't know the general direction that you need to go. I keep a map in my vehicle, because it gives me an understanding of the direction I need to be going. I become familiar with that direction so that if perchance I get sent in the wrong direction I will recognize it right away.

Drs. Steve Parr and Tom Crites, two of our very fine Georgia Baptist Mission Board staff, have teamed up once again, as they did in writing the highly acclaimed volume, *Why They Stay*. This book, *Pivot Points,* presents fascinating and informative research on 74 Georgia Baptist churches that excelled across the board in the five qualities identified by Georgia Baptists as essential to healthy churches. These include: Spiritual Renewal, Kingdom Generosity, Church Revitalization, Church Planting, and Authentic Evangelism. A comparative study of several hundred other churches was utilized to identify key differences between churches that are thriving and churches that are not. Nine vital issues faced by our churches were examined with a focus upon the pastor as the key leader.

Our pastors are hearing multiple voices offering guidance today. These voices at times contradict. So, it's easy to become confused and misdirected in an effort to sharpen your leadership skills and to provide creative and innovative leadership for your church. Parr and Crites' book provides a roadmap for your ministry related to multiple key issues. You will learn what is actually working today among our churches that are excelling. Both biblically and experientially based, this book will offer practical guidance for you and your church.

Perhaps you have come to the place in your ministry when you realize a need to "recalculate." I believe this book will help you to do that as you strive to please the Lord and reach your maximum potential.

J. Robert White
Executive Director
Georgia Baptist Mission Board

INTRODUCTION

Weekends in autumn are awesome. Childhood memories of jumping into piles of leaves, sandlot stickball games with the kids in the neighborhood, and cool nights that call for a jacket come flooding back for most. This writer remembers riding a bicycle for hours through the neighborhoods with friends, looking for the next adventure. Meetings around an apple tree on an empty lot often turned into spontaneous competitions of knocking over tin cans and bottles with the fallen apples. Those apples would become hand grenades, baseballs, or bowling balls… they could transform into just about anything. If the season was right and the tree had a good year, one could enjoy eating an apple snapped right off the branch.

There seemed to be nothing better than stopping for a snack at the apple tree on a crisp afternoon, relishing the sweet crunch of the fruit. There was nothing worse than seeing that an apple had a worm living inside it. Well, maybe there was something worse—finding that half a worm was in the apple after taking the first bite! Apples are sneaky. They can look delicious on the outside yet be worm-infested on the inside. Many unsuspecting kids experienced a sneaky apple hiding a wiggly surprise. Many more found their seemingly perfect apple bruised, soft, and rotten on the inside.

In many ways, churches can be compared to apples. Many are bright, welcoming, shiny, and seemingly wonderful on the exterior, but are wormy, bruised, and damaged. Too many people have been tricked by the glossy gleam of facades and performances. In Georgia, an estimated four out of five Southern Baptist churches are in some state of degradation.[1] Some are downright infested. The problem is ubiquitous. Unless something changes, the American church will decline in health and vitality until its ultimate demise. Today's popular "solutions" for reviving local churches and partnerships are simply polishing the peel of our ever-softening apple. In reality, the issues are core issues, not peel issues.

New Ministry Reality

The new reality of American Churches is throwing its followers into an existential crisis. Church leaders know this to be true. They point to evidence noticed in the seismic trends emerging in the American religious landscape. These trends may well represent the largest short-term shift of religious thought in our nation's history and is certainly producing a new ministry reality.[2] This shift is evidenced in the realization that the systems we have become accustomed to and dependent upon are involved in mass organizational introspection. This existential crisis or identity crisis will continue to take shape over the next couple of decades as generational Builders and Boomers fade from our churches, and Millennials (born around 1985 to 2000) and the younger Generation Z (born around 2000 to present) emerge. The differences between these generations in religious thought, preferences, values, and patterns are in many ways chasms apart. These differences are creating spiritual, logistical, and missional challenges and opportunities.

Research indicates that this new wave of believers is not staying to fight for their place in church life; they are moving on. It could be that, at the moment, there is something deeper occurring in this sociological phenomenon. You probably remember the sense of optimism in the research. Thom Rainer suggests, "Although some young believers are moving away from church, many remain spiritually astute."[3] Christian Smith observed, "The religion and spirituality of most teenagers actually strike us as very powerfully reflecting the contours, priorities, expectations and structures of the larger adult world into which adolescents are being socialized."[4] Gabe Lyons and David Kinnaman found that young adults were interested in spirituality and specifically Jesus, but were having trouble seeing the connection to the modern church.[5]

In the nearly 10 years since the research and writing of these experts, the teens they studied have become adults. Since the time of their analysis, young adults are observed "cutting the cord" that tethered their culture to that of their parents, including the cultural ties of their faith to traditional expressions of their parents' faith. It seems that they are, in some sort of deconstruction phase, related to their personal perspectives about spirituality. The deconstruction manifests itself in some young Christians as a search for, to them, a purer expression of Christianity. Some have described this as a young adult's attempt at finding a spiritual "center." They feel that Millennials are peeling away the externals of the church to discover the anchor that helps them live the lives they are living.[6] It is as if they have bitten into a wormy apple and decided to cut down the apple tree, hoping to discover relevance. They are trying to comprehend where faith applies to their lives. This search for a significant moment is in response to their perceptions of a church that is culturally and spiritually irrelevant, therefore, opening the door to deconstruction of traditional praxis and, in some cases, orthodoxy.[7]

How does a pastor respond? The first reaction is to polish the peel. Should our church build a bigger building, creating a local buzz that may attract members from other churches? Should we polish up the peel with new music and better lighting? These quick fixes do not address the core issues. Consider the following exploration into various strategic considerations, as we seek God for His direction in these times.

Why This, Why Now?

Discipleship was the greatest need identified by our research. This was not defined as a program or a class at church, but discipleship as a *relationship*. In the next several sections, you will discover foundational issues, which fuel the motivations, attitudes, and perceptions of biblical discipleship. This is more important than ever given recent church trends, and it must start with Generation Z. We must prepare the younger generations to take the mantle of church and kingdom leadership. Currently, homes and churches are filled with children and teenagers that can be influenced now. Reversal of recent trends may be accomplished by equipping and releasing healthy, sincere, and committed young believers into the world. Every effort must be made now to impart a faith through an authentic relationship with the living God. The next generation must be prepared and empowered for a distinctly Christian and kingdom lifestyle as they go out into the world. In many churches this will require a completely different direction, tone, and approach in their discipleship ministries.

The American church is in crisis. Baptists have enjoyed a delay in the downward trends that other denominations have experienced, but that is no longer the case. Efforts to find a solution to the problems are increasing and stirring angst. The timing is right to make a change in the system.

Summary

The information you will find in this report is part of the solution to this growing problem. You will read about significant differences in nine issues where the attitudes, motivations, and priorities of the pastors in some of the most impressive churches in our state are compared to the typical Georgia Baptist church pastor. The pastors and churches you read about are not perfect. All have issues and problems, but they are thriving in the midst of the changing American culture. You will see pastors that are leading their church to give generously and take initiative.

GIVE GENEROUSLY

CHAPTER ONE
GENEROSITY

For God so loved the world, He gave…

Pastors in this study indicated generosity is in the DNA of the members. This was significantly different from the typical church we studied. Keep in mind, some experts predict a slow and grinding attrition in church membership over the next few decades. "The current church institutional landscape, barring a miracle or unprecedented revival, will radically decline and change over the next few decades… some institutional churches will continue to consolidate members and resources while most institutional churches slowly atrophy and die."[8] While general church predictions are alarming, they reveal a deeper issue. *Attrition in giving* may be far more accelerated and significant, manifesting as ministry recession, reduction, and contraction. Gary Bulley, church strategist and international leader, highlights the issue:

> "Just as older generations are more committed to church attendance, so too are they more committed to giving. Builder Christians (65 years and older) give to church on average 3.22% of their income, while Millennial Christians give just .8%. Builders, on average, likewise have higher levels of wealth on which to give than do Millennials. This results in Builders currently providing 46% of church

budgets, while Millennials give less than 4% of church budgets."[9]

You may be saying to yourself, "That makes sense. The older members of the church have more to give than the younger members of the church." But it is not just that they have more to give; the issue is they are giving a higher percentage of their incomes than younger generations.

Percent Given by Age

Age	Percent Given
65+	46
55-64	22
45-54	17
35-44	11
-35	4

Blackbaud's Target Analytics Nonprofit Cooperative Database.

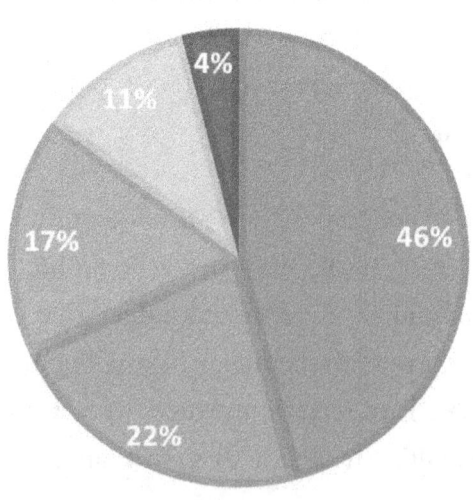

PERCENTAGE OF TOTAL RELIGIOUS GIVING

Understand this disparity: the Builder generation is giving 46% of the total net dollars given to churches and religious organizations. Their children, the Boomers, are giving roughly half, 22%, of their net total. Boomers, once the largest and most successful generation to ever exist, give half of the amount of their parents. Hence, the Boomers will not replace the gifts that their parents are currently giving as their patterns are already established. Most are retiring and settling into fixed incomes. The net giving of the once largest generation has reached its peak.

Digging deeper into the issue of giving reveals 68% of current giving is by people 55 and older. If nothing changes, religious giving will drop by one-half in the next 14 years and may continue a more precipitous negative trend after. Additionally, the independent spirit seen flickering in Boomers' giving is burning bright in subsequent age groups as they continue to give relatively little. Bulley shares, "Much is being made today about the reluctance of Millennials to support church budgets. The overarching theme is that Millennials do not believe in supporting institutional church expressions and the buildings and staff that go with them.

They generally prefer to direct giving towards compassion ministries and causes they are personally invested in."[10] Young adults are bearing fruit of the attitudes planted in their hearts as they watched their parents and grandparents give.

Of course, a decline in giving will greatly accelerate if laws are changed or adjusted to negatively impact charitable tax exemptions for religious giving. In addition, the offering "pie" could suddenly become smaller if churches are required to use a portion to pay property taxes. How might a church adjust support for pastors and clergy should they be required to pay taxes on housing allowances? Any or all of these scenarios are not hard to imagine in a new American reality.

Surely these changing and impactful factors are simply "sky falling" sentiment, right? Are we not hearing common testimony pointing to a stable giving climate at the local church level? Aren't gifts to the local associations strong? Isn't there a steady cooperative partnership? Offerings are going up, aren't they? No, they are not. The table on the next page tracks the historical giving trends of Georgia Baptist churches between 2000 and 2016. For the most part, total net receipts have been steadily increasing. Compared to 15 years ago, Georgia Baptists give a quarter of a billion more through their churches. That is good news until the dollars are adjusted for inflation. In today's dollars, the total value of the 2015 offerings given by Baptist churches in Georgia are worth $50,000,000 less than the total value of the offerings given in 2000 because of inflation.

Those dollars translate into ministry. In our state, we have basically lost the ability to do about 5% of our ministry. Understand, if nothing changes for the better and things do not get any worse, then we can expect to be doing two-thirds of what we do reaching the lost, teaching our children, and ministering to the needy in 18 years. That means one-third less churches, one-third fewer pastors, and one-third less ministry in less than 20 years.

Year	Total Net Receipts[11]	Member Per Capita Giving	Annual Per Capita Income[12]	Percentage of Income Given	Per Capita Gift Adjusted for Inflation[13]
2000	$783,433,983	$574.17	$22,346.00	2.57%	$805.00
2001	$842,353,137	$611.45	$22,851.00	2.68%	$833.55
2002	$893,872,311	$649.85	$22,794.00	2.85%	$872.11
2003	$909,999,872	$661.65	$23,276.00	2.84%	$868.16
2004	$959,738,197	$687.08	$23,857.00	2.88%	$878.14
2005	$1,006,385,688	$718.00	$25,036.00	2.87%	$887.58
2006	$1,029,001,160	$738.91	$26,352.00	2.80%	$884.89
2007	$1,085,430,305	$780.04	$26,804.00	2.91%	$908.27
2008	$1,069,131,645	$773.26	$26,964.00	2.87%	$867.09
2009	$1,043,053,766	$752.98	$26,530.00	2.84%	$847.36
2010	$1,016,641,389	$727.34	$26,558.00	2.74%	$805.30
2011	$1,025,589,423	$729.35	$27,554.00	2.65%	$782.81
2012	$1,029,585,881	$727.26	$28,281.00	2.57%	$764.75
2013	$1,013,783,026	$721.04	$30,027.00	2.40%	$747.26
2014	$1,033,913,393	$734.91	$30,176.00	2.44%	$749.91
2015	$1,042,618,663	$763.09	$31,653.00	2.41%	$777.29

Dr. J. Robert White, Executive Director of the Georgia Baptist Mission Board, has lamented over these facts. Recently, he shared what he felt was at the heart of the issue: "Some of our pastors are not teaching on tithing, because many of them are not tithers." Could part of the solution to this devastating local and national issue rest in the unrepentant hearts of our pastors?

What has happened to all of our givers? Pastors of churches that were in the top 2% in our study stated, "our church is full of givers." There was a significant difference in their perceptions compared to those that were not in the group. Giving records back up their claims as the top church's attendees gave per capita roughly 17.2% more than all the other attendees in Georgia Baptist churches. A couple of things that surfaced from the study are worth examining. Pastors of the vibrant churches stated that their church had a strong benevolence ministry, and they were not afraid to talk about tithing in their church. These perceptions are expressions of a corporate attitude of generosity.

As a researcher, I am taught to seek to understand the truth. Therefore, I can only understand this issue through the lens of my own experiences. Giving, to me, is more than an act of obedience; it is an act of love. Personally, I never knew what it meant to give until I fell in love. It seemed as if the giving of a flower, candy, or a ring was an extension of what I was feeling in my heart. I couldn't wait to give. I stood holding my bride's hand before God, my family, and my closest friends and vowed to give myself away. I endowed all my worldly goods and dedicated my future life to this woman I loved. She did the same; everything she was and everything she would become she offered to me as a token of the love in her heart. That day was a profound, sacred, and vulnerable moment in my life. It was a picture of the love relationship God desires with me. God has given me His all. In love, my response should be to reciprocate by offering all to Him.

When a man determines not to give, he is revealing his true heart. As you read this, you may be experiencing some negative feelings regarding the topic. There seems to be an "under-the-surface" consensus that pastors should not discuss giving, because it is a private matter between God and the individual. I have also heard some express aversion toward the teaching of a tithe. Some consider it legalistic to instruct people to tithe, feeling that "the Old Testament taught the law of tithing, whereas the New Testament teaches the grace of giving." I believe that when God instructed man to tithe and further to give graciously above the tithe, He revealed a miraculous mechanism through which His glory is revealed.

Donald Whitney has placed it neatly inside this nutshell: "How we use money for ourselves, for others, and especially for the sake of God's kingdom is from first to last a spiritual issue."[14] For man, the act of tithing makes a number of spiritual statements. These statements are made first to God, to oneself, and finally, to others.

When I tithe, I affirm to the Lord, "You own me." Sometimes, I forget that my worldly goods are really God's possessions. I trick myself into believing that I have worked hard to make things my own. The truth is, "The earth and everything in it, the world and its inhabitants, belong to the LORD." (1 Corinthians 10:26 HCSB) I own nothing. God has entrusted me with a portion of His "everything" to manage. I am merely a steward of a tiny bit of His vast wealth. I am invited to enjoy some of that which He allows me to manage, so the question is not "how much of my money do I give to God's work?" but "how much of God's money do I keep for myself?" The fact that I am instructed to keep and personally use 90% of the Lord's money is wondrously gracious. Furthermore, He blesses my faithfulness by increasing my tiny bit, allowing me to enjoy more of that which is His.

Another statement I make to the Lord when I tithe is, "You deserve my worship." Giving a tithe of the money God allows us to manage is an act of worship. It reflects my understanding of who God is. If I had no regard for God or did not believe that He is who He says

He is, then I may not be as motivated to tithe. Giving is an act of worship that is pleasing to the Lord (Philippians 4:18). Giving is a part of this miraculous mechanism He has created for His glory. Consider this: God assigns us stewardship of a bit of His creation. Then, He instructs us to give a small percentage in an act of worship that in return blesses the giver. The gift, the act of giving, and the blessing are designed to all return to the benefit of the steward. For that alone, God deserves my worship.

I also say, "You have my trust" when I tithe. A biblical illustration of this statement is seen in Mark 12, as the offering Jesus brought to the attention of His disciples was that of a woman who placed two small coins into the receptacle. Jesus said it was worth more than all the other offerings, because it was everything she had. The woman was expressing her trust in God to provide her needs. She could have held back one of the coins, and who could have blamed her? It probably could have bought her a small loaf of bread or a handful of olives. She could have kept both coins, and probably no one would have missed her gift as the treasure was counted. But she gave both of them in an act of faith, trusting God to take care of her. Comparing my giving to her's is embarrassing. She gave it all; I give a small percentage. Yet, there have been times when I have anxiously given, wondering how I would "make ends meet." Tithing is a small way that I say to God, "I trust You." Remember Paul's joyous words to the Philippians, "My God shall supply all your need according to his riches in glory by Christ Jesus." (Philippians 4:19 KJV) Their giving was an act of faith, a blessing to Paul, and yet even more a "fragrant offering, an acceptable sacrifice to God."

Personal affirmations arise when we tithe. We tell ourselves, "I want to be blessed." God promises that He will bless the giver. He invites man to personally experience His faithfulness when He says, "Test Me in this way." (Malachi 3:10 HCSB) God will not fail His own test. Don't miss this powerful truth: When I decide to tithe, I am affirming my desire to be blessed.

We also affirm our desire to be used by God in His work. Understand, God really does not need you. He can do everything He needs to do without your help. Sorry to bust your balloon, but His work will continue without your help. So, considering the opportunity to join God in His work, man says to himself, "I want God to use me." I was reminded of this very truth as I watched a potter throw a beautiful pot. The artist moved the clay using a variety of unpretentious tools. Some tools smoothed the surface of the clay, knives trimmed, and brushes stained. Each was used for a specific purpose. Each tool is a simple, anonymous part of the wondrous process. Imagine for a moment one of the scrapers saying to the artist, "Do not use me today, I wish to stay in my drawer." As ridiculous as that may seem, that is what we basically say to the Lord if we decide not to tithe. On the other hand, we express our desire to be used in His work when we give. When we give, it opens the door for God to speak to others. I have heard numerous testimonies from people who were down to the last dime, or wondering where they would find the money to buy formula for the baby, only to have God provide at just the right moment. I have seen the hungry fed and the homeless clothed through the gifts of my church. I have seen the eyes of a child sparkle as she placed a new coat around her shoulders, while her mother cried tears of joy and relief. I have seen men receive Christ after receiving basic medical care. It seems that in each of these instances, a mother, child, father, or son had prayed for God's intervention into their lives and circumstances. Through the ministry made possible by our tithes and offerings, other people understand, "God is real and He loves them."

Sometimes we miss out on the chance to share with some of the poor and needy in our mission fields, because we give with the wrong motive. I have seen leaders determine benevolence based upon the potential return on the "investment." Recently, I heard of a church that suspended a ministry to a mobile home community, because they had not had any of the parents of the children in the community join the church. Membership felt that the time, energy, and money spent in the community was "a huge waste." I shared that I was happy there was a church in a Chicago suburb a few years back that did not feel the same way. Someone in that church picked up a little girl each week for Sunday School and each summer for Vacation Bible School. The people of that church shared the love of Jesus with her, knowing that her mom and dad may not ever darken the door of the worship center. That little girl trusted Jesus during VBS one summer and learned how to love the Lord in that church. Had someone considered the time, energy, and money spent on reaching her "a huge waste" I would not be writing this report for you, as that little girl was my mother. Generous givers give, understanding that God never wastes a gift.

In summary, I recently celebrated the birthday of my son as he turned 23 years old. As I reflected upon the time, energy, prayers, and, yes, money invested in him, I found that it was all worth it. I am so blessed to see the people my children are becoming. I do not regret anything. We will all have this type of profound and powerful moment as we reach the ends of our lives. We will all have the moment when we consider our legacies and our impact. However, I guarantee that none of us will regret tithing and giving offerings to the Lord's work. We will all wish we had the opportunity to do more.

What do you do with this information? Vibrant churches have generosity in their DNA. How does that happen? It begins with leadership. The attitude of the pastor, staff, and key leaders sets the tone for everyone else. Are you personally generous in your giving? Are you disciplined in your giving? Are you a good steward of what God has blessed you with? Are you modeling good money management? Are you teaching and affirming money management? Do you shy away from discussing or teaching about tithing and stewardship? If it is not part of your DNA as a leader, it is highly unlikely to be in the DNA of the members. Remember that what the leader elevates is where followers gravitate.

Pastor, will you receive this challenge? I believe it is your responsibility to lead your people to give. At the beginning of this chapter I asked, "What has happened to all our givers?" I believe they are there, much like sheep following the shepherd to a muddy stagnant pool, while the clear, refreshing stream lies just beyond. Lead your flock to give generously. Lead them to give expecting nothing in return. Pastor, lead your flock in giving; then boldly teach them to tithe and see if God will not "throw open the floodgates of heaven and pour out so much blessing that you will not have enough room for it." (Malachi 3:10)

CHAPTER TWO
INTENTIONALITY

Leading a church to be vibrant and effective is no easy task. One common approach to addressing this difficult task is to imitate the leadership of other prominent churches. Feeling the heavy burden of a lifeless church, a leader may turn his attention to experts esteemed as radical and daring, hoping to uncover the secret to church "success." Consequently, frustrated pastors looking for anything to fix their church, "buy in" to a franchise mentality, promising life, power, and hope for their church. Sometimes, a well-meaning pastor attends a conference where certain churches are spotlighted. Then, energized by the possibility of leading a congregation like the spotlight church, the pastor attempts to mimic qualities, traits, and characteristics of these prominent churches. This is often followed by a negative response from institutionalized members who push back against the proposed changes. Many times, if the pastor remains at the church, he starts the cycle over, looking for anything that will help him lead his church. The pastor is both well-meaning and perpetually frustrated.

Our research found pastors in thriving churches approaching ministry differently. Part of the purpose of this study was to uncover some of the underlying motivations behind what churches and pastors do. We discovered that pastors in vibrant churches do not seek to imitate the newest version of a popular church. Yes, they may do some of the same things that many spotlight churches do. They are keen at observing and applying what they learn from other effective leaders. They appear, however, to possess a motivation that is significantly different than many other church leaders. They place a high priority on intentionally reaching out to their community. As a matter of fact, this issue rated the highest score when we looked at how thriving churches and other churches differed.

As you are reading this, you may be saying to yourself, "We are good on this issue." However, the importance of this issue demands honest self-reflection. Consider this picture: the typical Georgia church has a number of ministries and programs focused on a variety of age groups. They have a comfortable worship space, plenty of parking, clean preschool areas, as well as Kool-Aid and cookies for the kids. Just about anyone who walks through the doors of any church will be welcomed by at least a few people. The Sunday services are many times meaningful and fulfilling to all present. A typical preacher will see smiling faces enter the front door each Sunday morning and shake several hands and slap several backs, as the people leave at noon or soon thereafter. Is that a familiar picture? There is nothing wrong with anything in that description, but the churches that are thriving do everything mentioned plus prioritize reaching out to the community.

Notice everything in the description above was focused on the gathering of God's people. The activities were located at the church, and the focus was the church building and church property. Yes, anyone would be welcomed if they came to the church, but that is the problem. They would have to come to the church. Thriving churches make every effort to highlight the time when the congregation is gathered on Sundays, but they are even more focused on the time the congregation is scattered into their neighborhoods during the rest of the week. They focus on reaching out to the community so much, it becomes a "brand" of the church.

What do I mean by a "brand" of the church? If I were to come to your community and start asking people in the neighborhood about your church, I would soon learn a lot about your brand, reputation, or what your church is known for. I have often stopped at a local gas station, many times just blocks from the church, to test my hypothesis. There have been times when I asked for directions and the clerk would say, "I don't know where that church is." I remember the day I walked to a drug store to buy a Diet Coke and asked a young lady where the local church was. She had no idea even though the steeple could be seen through the front windows. Would that young lady have known the church better had they been focused on reaching out to the community? You better believe it. What a blessing to find a clerk who knows the church and talks highly of the members and pastor. "They really care about our community," is an awesome testimony from a mailman, nurse at the local emergency room, or a teacher at the school down the street. That is a powerful church brand. Positive or negative, good or bad, every church has a brand. Thriving churches intentionally reach out to the community to the point that they are known by their caring brand.

How have these churches established such a powerful brand? They have considered the time when the congregation is scattered (not at the church on a Sunday morning) as important to the outreach and ministry of the church as the time when the congregation is gathered on each Sunday. A wise pastor will understand this is an enormous shift in our culture. In the past it has been said, "If you build it, they will come." I am unsure if the phrase was stolen from the *Field of Dreams* movie, or if the movie stole it from church growth experts; but, at any rate, it has been a church growth mantra for years. Congregations have sought to build campuses that were guest friendly, inviting, and pleasing. Facilities were designed to attract families and community members to the church property. That approach is the equivalent of a fisherman expecting the fish to come to the boat instead of taking the boat to where the fish are. Church leader and strategist, Gary Bulley shares some general reasons why we must empower the church and advance the kingdom in coming decades.

> "First, the general anti-institutional inclinations of Millennials (ages 18 to 35) in particular indicate we cannot expect to see them in large numbers in our church gatherings any time soon. They are also highly educated, under-employed, and heavily in debt. Thus, many are simply hustling to get by and they indicate they do not have the time or resources to invest in church institutions.
>
> While many Millennials are open to Christianity, they remain closed to institutional expressions of Christianity they view as irrelevant, restrictive, antiquated, intolerant, dysfunctional, or destructive.
>
> Second, (current) Christians demonstrate lower commitment to the church institution, and by association, the church gathered. Church is now what you do when

you don't have anything else to do on Sunday. Many well-meaning members must regularly choose between a variety of important functions on Sunday. That church is often relegated to the back burner is disappointing, but consistent. Regardless, one or two Sundays per month is not enough to empower members and attenders to have a vibrant spiritual life."[15]

Current trends show a decrease in the number of people regularly attending church services, as well as a decrease in the frequency of attendance of church members. These facts alone should encourage a pastor to intentionally reach out into the community, but consider this: only one-third of religiously unaffiliated people say they attend a service *ever*.[16] That means a lost person is not likely to appear in your service. To illustrate this point, consider this: of the total 1,000 people living around your church, 800 do not attend church on a regular basis, 400 are not affiliated with a particular religious group or belief, 133 would consider attending a church service on Easter, Christmas, or for a funeral, and 50 would lean toward a Protestant religious service over a Catholic service. In total, roughly five percent of the population around any particular church might, by chance, visit your church on Easter, Christmas, or for a funeral. To be honest, bigger and better does little in the current culture to encourage unchurched people to experience worship in your church.

Consider this: church is a relationship, not a product. Pastors in our study get this concept. They develop people and especially their leaders for a natural and organic ministry in the community. Church leaders should transition their roles to empowering the people of the church for ministry in the marketplaces and tribes of the community. Our churches should be places where the congregation gathered is inspired, encouraged, equipped, and empowered. We should become equipping centers that empower people to practically answer four important questions for their lives.

Where (or who) in my world is my ministry? Pastor, are you training your people to think like a missionary? Help them to see that God has placed them in their context for a purpose. Help them to see the lostness in the community. Lead them to face the heartbreaking realities that exist in their neighborhoods and communities. Lead them to pray for opportunities to share the love of Jesus in their own special mission field. Help each of your members locate a place in the community where they can make a difference. Challenge them to get into the dirt and muck of the community. Lead them to volunteer at a prison, or a school, or a hospital, or a nursing home. Whether it is helping a family down the street or working at a soup kitchen downtown, help them to find where they are a missing piece of the puzzle.

Who is discipling me and who am I discipling? This is an issue that cannot be left alone. For whatever reasons, the typical Southern Baptist church has struggled to disciple its members for at least two generations. Take an honest look around your congregation. Are there many people that are being discipled? Are you discipling anyone? Lead your church to develop a culture of discipleship where one believer disciples another believer who disciples another believer and so on.

With whom am I having spiritual (evangelistic) conversations?

Do you remember the day when people would share about divine appointments? Recently I sat in a Starbucks in the Augusta Mall with my brother and daughter. I noticed a young lady carrying a Bible and gave her a "thumbs up" sign and pointed to her Bible. She took her place at the table right next to us. She seemed to be listening to everything that we were saying. My daughter gave her a grin, which she took as an invitation to join the conversation. After a couple of minutes, she shared how she recently received the Bible from her aunt who had since passed away. She turned to Revelation 4, where several pages were torn out and missing. She asked if we knew what had been torn out. Talk about a door swung wide open! We talked and listened to this young lady. I shared the gospel with her and she was ready to receive it. God had placed us in that moment, in that appointed time for this conversion. What a blessing and honor to be there for that moment.

Pastor, encourage your people to prepare for the moments God is preparing for them. Teach them to look for the opportunities to have spiritual conversations. Teach them what a spiritual or an evangelistic conversation looks like. Teach them how to depend on the Holy Spirit's leadership and equip them with resources that will prepare them for the conversations.

How can the church help me do these things? Influencing the mindset of your congregation in more of an outward focus takes time, energy, and resources. You will need to remind your members constantly to be the "church scattered," as well as the "church gathered." They will need to hear your challenges from the pulpit. They will need to hear personal testimonies in small groups and Bible studies. They will need to have access to resources to help with questions and to offer ideas. They will need to be reminded to pray, pray, pray! And that is just to start.

Remember, thriving churches make every effort to highlight the time when the congregation is gathered on Sundays, but they are even more focused on the time the congregation is scattered into their neighborhoods. Make every effort to develop a brand that says "We love our community."

CHAPTER THREE
VITALITY

Have you ever been in a lifeless worship service? Boy, I have. I remember being in a recent service that was basically on life-support. The people seemed uninspired and defeated, at least a half dozen were ready to nod off to sleep, the atmosphere was depressing, the preaching dull. I could have probably gathered up all my things and simply made my way out the side door with almost no one noticing. I let my mind drift to consider lunch plans. I checked the clock for the tenth time to see that time had mysteriously slowed to a curious halt. I pondered how much longer the service would last ... oh the agony. Mentally, I planned my escape, wondering if my wife, Cyndy, would be able to understand the single eyebrow raised signal that would mark the moment to move out. Anxiously, I counted the seconds, wrestling, "Should I stay or should I go?" A decision had to be made, and "This could not go on much longer!" I thought. I would have bolted in a rush of relief if only ... I was not in the middle of delivering the sermon.

All kidding aside, this is a real issue in some churches. Too many churches are sick, dying, or dead, and sometimes do not even know it. David Olson shared the facts with us a few years ago.[17] Through a study using a national database of over 200,000 churches, he identified eroding church attendance, eroding total number of churches, and eroding levels of church influence on local communities. Recent evaluators have unanimously indicated that North American church health is anemic.[18] 80-85% of the churches in America are in the final stages of their life cycle, decline, and death.[19] Some have suggested that only 11% of all churches are not in a plateau or a declining state.[20] Churches need vitality now more than ever. Pastors, desperate to find solutions for their stagnant and declining congregations, are trying any and every theory of church health appearing on the market. Unfortunately, the information they find is often not helpful, and adds to the issues present in the congregation, leading to greater levels of frustration for both the pastor and lay membership.

Some churches find seasons of life and joy and flourish in those times, but that is not as common as it should be. The pastors in our study described their worship services concerning the vitality of the congregation, and the expectancy of the people. The pastors that were leaders of vibrant churches felt that the levels of vitality were significantly different than the pastors of all the other churches. They identified several traits that pointed to some deeper factors. These pastors felt that their people were anticipating revival. They also believed that the services were consistently full of energy. They perceived that a current of expectancy flowed through most of the congregation as they gathered to see God at work. A unique passion and enthusiasm was evident in the gatherings of these churches.

It was not surprising that this issue emerged out of the research, especially having spent time with thousands of church leaders over the years. We were especially interested in the differences that existed in the two groups of churches. Of all the factors we saw in the study, the fourth and fifth top ranking factors applied to the issue of vitality. It was clear from our research that leaders of the vibrant churches experienced more vitality than the leaders of the other churches in the study. As mentioned earlier, one of the major purposes of this study was to understand the underlying factors that made the differences in this special group of churches. We wanted to see if we could peel back the surface and understand what the driving forces are at the heart of their ministries. This issue proved to be particularly helpful in understanding the underlying core issues.

First, leaders recognized the level of "energy" in a worship service as something that needed to be considered. Understanding that energy is the expression of a deeper feature is important in our reflection here. Energy flows. It comes from a source. A pastor who says to his worship leader, "We need to add more energy to our services" is missing the point. Energy is evidence that something else is happening. Dr. Jon Duncan, state missionary/specialist in Worship and Music Ministry of the Georgia Baptist Mission Board, recently conducted a survey of worship leaders and pastors and discovered that those studied felt that worship was best when it was as they described "joyous." When asked about this, he explained that a joy-filled service was evidence of a deeper feature. It was not a product that could be added to the order of worship. A worship experience full of joy could be realized no matter the location, size, style, or age of the congregation. It flowed from what the leaders and participants brought to the worship experience. Dr. Duncan was essentially talking about the same quality that our pastors highlighted in the study. Pastors in the study confirmed that when a larger number of the members spend personal time with God during the week, they come to expect God to move in the worship service on the weekend.

People that were close to God understood when He was at work and rejoiced in response to God's demonstration of grace. When a pastor talked about energy, he talked about the expectation, realization, and reflection of the work of God's Holy Spirit.

A lack of vitality in our churches is not a new problem. Church leaders have written about it for years. For example, Findley Edge wrote nearly 55 years ago, "At the present time, churches are experiencing a period of almost unparalleled popularity and prosperity. Such a situation normally would be the basis for unrestrained optimism and rejoicing. Strangely, such is not the case. Many thoughtful religious leaders and mature Christian laymen evidence a growing ferment of uneasiness and concern. In spite of plush church buildings, growing membership, and many vigorous activities that are carried on within the churches, something is seriously wrong with modern Christianity. Something is wrong at its center. It is in danger of losing its life and dynamic."[21] Since then, we have reached crisis level on this issue. The vast majority of church leaders are now experiencing the reality Edge was projecting. Their church has lost its vitality.

Now, before you jump to any conclusions and skip to the next chapter, consider what is being said here. Pastors of vibrant churches consistently saw energy in their services. They anticipated the movement of God. The people they led were expecting a revival. Why? The presence of authentic faith.

Authentic faith is a difficult topic to discuss today, as connotations of the word 'authentic' are sometimes tied to a personal perception of reality. What we are talking about here is a quality of faith that is uniquely God-focused. It begins with God's act of grace in salvation and continues in His invitation into a personal relationship. The tragic truth is there are many who have grown up attending our churches hearing about God that do not have a personal, vibrant relationship with Him. Why is vitality so difficult to find and so hard to maintain? One must consider three elements implicit within the idea of an authentic faith evidenced by vitality. Reflecting a bit on Edge's foundational work, *A Quest for Vitality in Religion* helps one to begin to understand the subtleties. Vitality comes from an authentic faith that is complete, surrendered, and purposeful.[22]

There are a few things a pastor should focus upon to build a foundation for vitality. First, a pastor must present a clear gospel message, teaching that Jesus' life, death, and resurrection is the *only* way to salvation. God's perfect plan to save the soul of man is completed through the shed blood of Christ. Apart from the knowledge of the gospel message, one cannot experience the true seed of vitality. Today, a spirit of practical universalism prevails over some congregations. Generally, there is no urgency in our church membership to share the gospel with their lost neighbors. Many are no longer burdened to share their faith with friends and family. This is practical universalism. Many of our people that sit in our pews every Sunday are not convinced that their friends, family, neighbors, and coworkers are going to hell without Jesus. They are not motivated to share the saving faith, because they do not understand that Jesus is the only way. Pastor, unapologetically preach the gospel, clear and unaltered! Lead church members to accept it entirely and without compromise. Teach them to live full and alive in the knowledge of the perfect, complete salvation plan of the Lord.

Second, direct the believers under your leadership to surrender their lives to God's sovereignty. This is an issue of discipleship. Believers must experience the joy and peace of a life surrendered to God's will. Maybe one of the best things you can do to help your followers understand how to remain in a surrendered growing relationship with God is to lead them through a study of Henry Blackaby's *Experiencing God*. Of course, there are other studies on knowing and doing the will of God, but this is one of the best. Your people will soon learn that "We don't choose what we will do for God; He invites us to join Him where He wants to involve us."[23] You will see the vitality in their lives when they move past just knowing about God to having an active relationship with God. A person seeking the sovereign Lord and His will comes to understand that He loves them, He has big plans for them, and they can be used to bring glory to Him. Spiritual vitality flows from a heart surrendered to the sovereignty of God.

Third, help them to see that God has a unique purpose for each of their lives. Sometimes, it is easier to consider the people that come to your church as a group—the congregation. God called us the "body" for a reason; to show us a little more about His plans. We are part of the body, each with a role to play. Not all of us are ears or eyes, as Paul explained to the Corinthians.[24] We all have special gifts given to us by the Holy Spirit for use in God's kingdom. Each individual brings a history of memories and experiences, a wealth of talents and abilities, and a context prepared by the Lord. It is within that wonderful complexity that God reveals His unique purpose, for each of His children. When your members begin to thrive in their unique purpose they will overflow with spiritual vitality.

Vibrant churches are full of people who are experiencing spiritual vitality led by passionate leaders. It begins with God, flows through the leaders, and infects the members. Lead your congregation to experience God and to discover their unique purposes, and you will find yourself in an energetic, vibrant church.

CHAPTER FOUR
EMPOWERING MEMBERS

I once heard the story of a husband and wife celebrating 25 years of marriage. The day of their anniversary, the husband arrived home after work to find his wife greeting him at the door.

She said, "Do you know what day it is?"

He replied, "Yes, it is our twenty-fifth anniversary."

With a surprised smile coming across her face she asked, "Did you get me a present?"

The man took her by the hand and answered, "Yes, I did. I bought you the most practical gift a loving husband could buy his perfect wife. I have bought you a burial plot. It is in the most prestigious cemetery in town, overlooking the lake where ducks come daily to enjoy the peace and serenity of the beautiful location. It was not cheap either. But, I knew that I would spare no expense for this year is a special one in our marriage."

As his wife's smile faded she swallowed and then spoke. "Well, that is a very practical gift. I appreciate you thinking about our future and I like it."

A year later, the couple sat at the breakfast table, and again the wife spoke up, "Do you know what day it is?"

The husband looking above his coffee cup stated, "Yes, it is our twenty-sixth wedding anniversary." The wife curiously asked, "Did you get me a gift?"

"A gift!?" the husband replied, "You didn't use the gift I bought you last year."

Seriously, the problem with many churches today is that people are not using their gifts in service of the Lord. Many people in church pews ignore the opportunities to operate in their own special way, using their God-given, unique abilities. The most vibrant churches in our study invited people to serve and released them to find their place of ministry. As a matter of fact, empowering and equipping members to serve is a high priority for the pastors of these special churches.

The pastors in our study identified several areas related to this issue, where there were significant differences in their perspectives compared to churches at large. First, the vibrant church pastor purposely *shares* the ministry load by equipping and releasing members to serve. Notice the nuance of the statement: the pastor shares the ministry. In many churches, pastors or staff do a pretty thorough job covering all the key responsibilities of the ministry. They preach and teach, maintain all the administrative duties, organize all the special events, and perform all the ministry tasks. This can be unhealthy.

A pastor can feel the pressures of all that responsibility and burn out. They can neglect their families, creating pressures at home. They inadvertently produce a codependent membership that views them more like a caretaker and less like a leader. This could be called micromanaging the ministry. It probably grows out of the fear of something falling apart or a job going undone. To some, it is easier to do all the work themselves than to equip others to do it properly. The root of this attitude is fear of failure.

Vibrant church pastors have discovered how to train and release their members to perform the ministry of the church. They have found that sharing responsibilities creates a healthy environment for the growth of those they lead.

Vibrant church pastors have an effective plan for making disciples. Discipleship of the believers is a challenging responsibility for the local pastor. It is a foundational task that supports all the other endeavors of the church. Remember how Paul commended the Thessalonians in the first chapter of his first letter to them. He said that they were imitating him. The word that he uses to describe discipleship here is tupos. Picture a person placing his stamp on his work, stating the identity of the craftsman that created the piece (1 Thessalonians 1:7). Paul wrote that the believers there became examples to the others. He went on to report that the influence of their lives was spreading world-wide. They were fulfilling the Great Commission, as they trained and discipled the believers in Thessalonica, Achaia, Macedonia, and literally everywhere Paul went. They had received the teachings of Paul and imitated him by discipling others who in turn discipled others and so on. Today, the simple and powerful truth of discipleship remains. Pastors who train disciples who train other disciples can reach the world. Vibrant church pastors have emphasized discipleship in their ministries.

In the top churches we studied, a couple key elements were part of a quality discipleship process. First, for almost every vibrant church, prayer and leading others to pray was a top priority, with a special emphasis on daily prayer. This is directly related to the prior two points. Prayer should undergird every aspect of a pastor's ministry. I fear that our culture has become overly pragmatic. Prayer has been moved to the back of their priority list. Maybe it is because some spend so much time doing ministry that there seems to be less time for praying. This is a real problem in many churches. Consider the typical church schedule. Members gather for a couple of hours on Sunday morning. They spend important time sharing about the blessings and challenges of the week. They open God's word and hear a sermon. They sing songs of the faith. And they pray. But how much prayer really takes place? Are we spending quality time going before the Father's throne with our requests and petitions? In many churches prayers are token rituals and have little or no impact on the service. In the worst cases, "prayer requests" devolve into gossip sessions. Vibrant church pastors felt that the prayer ministry of their church was effective and impactful. That does not happen by accident. Pastors who elevate prayer and lead their members to become people of prayer will have effective prayer ministries in their church. Vibrant church pastors encourage members to pray daily. That says a lot about these leaders. They truly believe that prayer makes a difference. They have seen God answer the prayers and find the people in their congregation growing in their faith, as they daily cry out to God.

Pastor, I want to challenge you to become a prayer warrior. Robert Anderson has served Georgia Baptists for years. He ministers to pastors in the hospital and in times of trouble. He is known as a prayer warrior. When asked how a pastor can become a prayer warrior, he said, "It begins and ends with prayer. Pastors must have a heart for prayer. He has to demonstrate the importance through a visible and dynamic prayer life." This type of ministry is "caught more than taught."

Anderson offers several steps to consider to get a prayer ministry started in your church. "Find the prayer warriors (and the potential prayer warriors) in the church. Try setting out a free book on prayer and invite people to take a copy if they are interested. Have them sign a list in exchange for the book and begin with these folks as your prayer group. Invite the group that took the books to in-depth training on prayer, cultivate them and lead them to pray."

In addition, Anderson shared, "Create venues for prayer, have people give prayer testimonies, and set aside times on the calendar for prayer emphases. This will help create an atmosphere of prayer in the church." Pastor, do not neglect the prayer ministry of the church.

Another key element we discovered in a vibrant church's discipleship process was the emphasis on relationship building. Vibrant church pastors have found that the relationships they are able to build with the people in their church are extremely important to the health of their church. One can see how this all ties together. Relationships are built through the discipleship of others. Pastors lead the people under their care to serve the church and pray. They are literally living life with others, developing bonds that make them feel like family. That is probably why believers call each other brother and sister. We are to be that close. It is difficult for a pastor to be vulnerable with people in his church. Sometimes, pastors feel pressure to keep up the appearance of one who has the perfect life and family. They are not supposed to be human, prone to mistakes and temptations. In an effort to lead, they allow relationships to develop at a safe distance. They never fully allow anyone close enough to help them grow. Insecurity is the driving force behind a pastor's need to keep these barriers. The pastors in our study felt the same pressures; and those that were in the most vibrant churches found a way to break through, allowing them to develop meaningful relationships with the people they serve.

Get a handle on what we are saying here, the top pastors in our study emphasized a discipleship process built upon two key elements; prayer and relationships. They grew with their members, realizing true discipleship and creating meaningful relationships in the process. They saw their members come alive in their faith, and the results were astounding. What can a pastor do to help make a difference in his church? Consider these few ideas as you think about empowering and equipping your people.

Develop a discipleship culture in your church. There are a growing number of resources available for today's pastor. I recommend using Robby Gallaty's resources.[25] Before a pastor can cultivate a culture of discipleship, he must clear up any ambiguity with the term. Sadly, we have many people using the same discipleship terms but speaking a different language. Thom Rainer and Eric Geiger define clarity as, "the ability of the process to be communicated and understood by the people ... If the process is not clearly defined so that everyone is speaking the same language, there is confusion and frustration."[26]

Define what you mean by making disciples. "Churches," according to author and disciple-maker, Bill Hull, "throw the word disciple around freely, but too often with no definition."[27] New Testament Professor Scot McKnight supports Hull's claim: "If one understands discipleship as 'daily routine,' then one will produce those who have daily routines. If one understands discipleship as 'evangelistic ministry,' then one will produce evangelists. If one understands discipleship as 'Bible study,' then one will produce biblical scholars. If one understands discipleship as 'effective operations,' then one will produce administrative geniuses."[28]

Furthermore, a quick survey of the Christian landscape will uncover various definitions of discipleship from different people. For example, Francis Chan defines discipleship differently than Bill Hull, author of *The Disciple-Making Pastor*. Jim Putman, pastor of Real Life ministries in Post Falls, Idaho, suggests a different approach than Alan Hirsch, founding director of *Forge Mission Training Network,* or even Derwin Gray, pastor of Transformation Church and author of *Limitless Life*. There is nothing wrong with the resources mentioned here; they are all valuable. They are mentioned as examples of the diverse definition of discipleship. We recommend that a pastor use these resources as he feels led, and contextualize his ministry the best he can.

Fortunately, Jesus, in His infinite wisdom, did not prescribe a model. Instead, He gave us a mandate: make disciples! He didn't suggest a process; He left us with principles, which is why Robert Coleman's book *The Master Plan of Discipleship* is timeless.

Ultimately, Jesus left the size of the group, the length of the group, and the particulars of the group up to the disciple-maker. But with great freedom comes great responsibility. One must decide on a system and faithfully follow. First, consider what discipleship is not. It's not a class, a seminar, a degree you earn, a program, or a 12-week Bible study. It's not a 40-day home group, a quick process, or a quick fix. It's not reserved for super Christians, and it is not an option!

We could say that discipleship is intentionally equipping believers with the Word of God through accountable relationships empowered by the Holy Spirit in order to replicate faithful followers of Christ. When people become disciples, they learn what Jesus said and live out what Jesus did (Matthew 28:19).

Did you catch the five components of a discipling relationship? A disciple is: intentional about equipping others for the work of ministry; studying/obeying the Word of God; accountable to other believers; empowered by the Holy Spirit; and reproducing what he was taught with others.[29] Determine that a top priority in your church will be to create a culture of discipleship.

Then you will be ready to release people to serve where they are led to exercise their gifts. Invite your congregation to join you in serving. Encourage them to think outside the church walls. Inspire them to look for ways to touch the community. Maybe they could volunteer to mentor kids at the local elementary school or to deliver hugs at a retirement center. They may see a playground that needs sprucing up or a housing development that needs paint. There is no better way to make a difference in the community than to send equipped and empowered people to serve it.

CHAPTER FIVE
EXCEPTIONAL LEADERSHIP

I once heard leadership guru John Maxwell say, "He who thinks he leadeth and has no one following, is only taking a walk." It is certainly true that there is no point in being a leader if no one is willing to follow. In our study of churches that are thriving in the midst of a changing culture, we noticed something about the pastors of the vibrant churches that stood out in contrast to our comparative sampling of churches. They were not effective simply because they had a title or because they had been called to serve the local church. They were not effective based on the level of education or the height of their seminary degree. Something set them apart from the pastors in the other churches.

One thing that is true about pastors is that they love the pulpit. For those that are called to preach there is no place more comfortable than standing in front of the congregation on Sunday morning proclaiming God's word. Preparing and presenting messages is both challenging and brings great joy. However, if simply preaching were the key skill needed in leading a congregation to thrive, then every congregation would be propelling forward and making an impact on their community. Every Sunday, every pulpit has a pastor who is preaching. Evidently, there is more to pastoral leadership than what happens in the pulpit.

Certainly, the pulpit can be used not only to preach the word of God but to communicate and inspire a congregation. However, congregations are not automatically inspired just because the preacher appears on the platform each Sunday morning. Here is what we discovered about the pastors in the most effective churches that set them apart.

Exceptional leadership is the focus of the pastor in a church that thrives in the midst of a changing culture. Let's think for a moment about the skills that a pastor needs to lead a congregation. Preaching skills and ability are important and make a definitive difference in moving a congregation forward. The pastors of thriving churches do not stop there. Additional examples of qualities needed to be effective as a pastor include people skills; time management skills; motivational skills (how to inspire people); team building skills; problem solving skills; conflict management skills; financial skills; staff development skills; volunteer enlistment skills; the ability to deal with difficult people; and etiquette. This list is by no means exhaustive.

Effective pastoral leadership is based on more than what happens behind the pulpit on Sundays. Ephesians 4:12 says, "and he himself gave some to be apostles, some prophets, some evangelists, and some pastors and teachers for the equipping of the saints for the work of ministry for the edifying of the body of Christ." [NKJV] Here is what we discovered in our research. The pastors of the thriving churches are *leadership junkies*. Perhaps you have played sports and are familiar with the term "gym rat." What is that? It is the athlete that is playing, practicing, and exercising day in and day out. He is always in the gym or on the field and not just when there is a formal or official practice going on. The "gym rat" lives to compete. That is essentially what we found out about the pastors in these thriving churches. Instead of being a "gym rat," these pastors are "leadership junkies."

What does it mean to be a "leadership junkie?" It means that they are intensely attentive to their personal leadership and the continued development of their leadership skills. They think about it frequently, talk about it often, and are very intentional about developing their own leadership and stretching their own abilities.

We noted one interesting observation. The pastors of these churches struggle with time to conduct outreach. But here is a good example of where the leadership comes in. They purposely equip others to spread the load. When we analyzed the data, we saw an interesting pattern. The leaders of the most thriving churches had prioritized leading over doing in several areas. Two examples included outreach to the community and ministry to the needs of members. In other words, they understand that outreach and ministry are both priorities. A church cannot possibly impact the community without these. More importantly, they understand that they cannot do it all by themselves. They are intentional about taking time to inspire, motivate, and equip others to be involved in outreach. Consider the wisdom of this approach. The members of the congregation come into contact with dozens, if not hundreds, of people each and every week that will never hear the pastor preach his sermon. The pastor of a thriving church approaches this from a leadership perspective. He asks the question, "How can I equip others to come alongside and proclaim the gospel; and minister to needs not just in the worship center on Sunday, but in the community throughout the week?"

Effective leaders equip and empower others to lead. Consider this example: Suppose a pastor is going to give five hours each week personally to conduct outreach. Most anyone would agree that such an effort would be commendable. What if he changed his approach? Suppose that instead of investing five hours in outreach he gave only three hours of personal time but invested the other two hours in equipping six other people to assist with outreach. Assume that the six he enlists are volunteers, and that his goal is to get them to invest at least one hour each week, in outreach, and evangelism. If four of the six volunteers come through and give an hour each week and you add that to the three hours the pastor continues to spend, the total invested in outreach will have increased from one person giving five hours to five people giving a total of seven hours each week. That may not sound like much. But what would happen in your church if 104 additional man hours of outreach sowing the gospel were invested in your community the coming year? That is the equivalent of what would result from this scenario.

To accomplish the task described requires wisdom, patience, commitment, and skill. It also requires skill to enlist those other six volunteers, motivate them to be involved in outreach, and equip others to interact and share the gospel. At this point we should acknowledge that not every pastor has equal leadership ability. Some are natural born leaders, and others have learned and developed their leadership over time. Others preach each Sunday but admittedly have little if any skill to inspire and move a congregation to make changes needed to thrive in the changing culture. While not everyone has equal leadership ability, every pastor can grow in his leadership skills.

How would you assess your own leadership journey? How influential and skilled are you in leading your congregation to thrive? Be reminded of the key point here: *exceptional leadership* is the focus of the pastor. They are leadership junkies.

Can a pastor grow and develop greater skills? Absolutely! Here are a few thoughts. First, spiritual dynamics cannot be ignored. The pastor needs God's anointing, resulting in the overflow of the Holy Spirit working in his life. That happens as he spends time personally alone with God day in and day out. Always remember that doing things for God is not the same thing as an intimate relationship with God. The overflow and anointing comes from that intimate, personal relationship that the pastor must attend to every day. Spend time in the Word of God and in prayer; and personally develop an intimate relationship with God.

If you grow spiritually but fail to grow in your skills as a leader, you will limit your influence and have a smaller number of followers than you desire to impact. On the other hand, if you develop your skills but you do not attend to your spiritual development, God's anointing will not be present, and the limitations will be even greater. Both your spiritual growth and your skills development must be given devoted attention. As an example, Paul reminded young Timothy to stir up the gift of God that was in him (2 Timothy 1:6). The gift that Timothy possessed came from God. But once Timothy received his gifts, he had the responsibility to stir them up. He needed to develop, sharpen, and enhance the gifts that God had given him.

Here are four things you can do to develop your leadership skills and exercise exceptional leadership:

Be knowledgeable of your gifts and strengths. What are your spiritual gifts? What are you really good at? What are your passions? You need to clearly understand your strengths, so that you can also know your weaknesses. For example, suppose a pastor admittedly lacks administrative gifts and struggles with organization. While it is not uncommon, it cannot be ignored. Affecting the culture and moving a group of people in the direction the congregation needs to go does require application of some organizational dynamics. It does require some degree of organization or administration. Some pastors are naturally gifted in administration while others struggle.

A pastor can be effective, whether he is strong in administration, ability or not. Here is the difference: a pastor that is lacking in administrative skills will bring people alongside him and will intentionally enlist others who have strong organizational and administrative gifts. Why? Because he knows it is a weakness for him. That is why it is important for you to understand and know your gifts and strengths. You need to be intentional in bringing people alongside you, whether volunteers or staff, who can complement and compensate for your weaknesses. Whatever the gifts, whatever the strengths, for a church to be effective people must be in positions of leadership that represent gifts and strengths in all areas.

No individual is good at everything. An effective pastor is very purposeful in knowing his gifts and strengths. Not only will he bring alongside those who can compensate for the gifts he does not possess, he will also develop skills himself. For example, if he is not strong in administration he may struggle with his own personal time management ability. The problem here is that if he fails or is weak in managing his time, he is going to undermine his own leadership.

Therefore, he must also improve his own abilities in terms of administrating or managing his own personal time.

Spend time with effective leaders. Would you agree that parents should be what they desire their children to become? Through years of observation and influence, children will ordinarily take on many qualities of their parents, whether positive or negative. Consider the same principle from a leadership perspective. You need to proactively seek to attach yourself to the leader you want to become. Identify leaders in effective churches and be intentional in spending time with them. It can be in an informal setting as simple as having lunch occasionally with another effective leader, or it can be a formal partnership, where you meet regularly for mentoring. You forfeit your right to lead at the point you fail to grow. No matter where you are in ministry, it is important that you attach yourself to effective leaders. If you are a young leader, you would do well to attach yourself to someone who is older and more experienced. If you are older, you would do well to attach yourself to a leader who is younger for reverse mentoring, so that you can continue to be stretched and effectively provide leadership for all generations.

Commit to be a life-long learner. That is not a unique concept, but it is something you will find to be particularly true of effective leaders. It has been said that leaders are readers. Why is that important? Because as you read, you are allowing other people to pour into your life. It is important that you read books on subjects related to leadership, as well as skills development. Refer back to the list mentioned earlier about skills needed by pastors. Reading books that relate to those subjects will serve you well in sharpening your skills. Make a commitment to be a life-long learner. What are you reading now? The fact that you are reading this speaks well for you and your leadership, but what is next? Conferences, seminars, and roundtables with other leaders are also important. You will observe that skilled pastors are not too proud to sit and learn from other leaders. Be sure that you are getting away, on some occasions, during the course of the year to attend something that improves your leadership and helps you develop your skills.

Commit to be a leader of leaders. Honestly, anyone can be a leader of followers. But, when you determine to become a leader of leaders, you will continually be compelled to sharpen your skills. You will have to step up, grow, and increase your knowledge if you are going to be a leader to leaders. In reality, developing leaders is the primary call of a leader. Are you being purposeful in enlisting and developing other leaders? Is that not what Jesus did? As God in the flesh, He certainly had all of the knowledge, authority, and ability to do what was needed. However, He was purposeful in calling apart 12 whom He called apostles, and He poured His life into them to help them become leaders also. They were good examples of attaching themselves to someone they wanted to be more like, as they observed the life of Jesus. That is what effective pastors do. They are leadership junkies. Exceptional leadership is their focus.

TAKE INITIATIVE

CHAPTER SIX
TACKLING PRIORITIES

Do you personally know a pastor in a church that is thriving? They are often admired for their skill in leading their church to progress, as the people grow in their faith and the community is touched by their ministry. The congregation is doing well, people are coming to faith, the church is growing, and they often seem to have it all together. Actually, that is not the reality.

Our research revealed the following surprise: the pastors leading the thriving churches in a changing culture wrestle with priorities. They don't necessarily have it all together. For example, we noticed that when pastors rank their priorities, outreach is almost always at or near the very top of their list. On the other hand, when we asked the pastors to describe how they actually spend their time, they do not spend as much time on outreach as they do many other things that are ranked much lower. In other words, they do not give as much time to outreach as suggested by their own stated priorities. To be clear, the suggestion is not that they are disingenuous or purposefully misleading, but that there is something deeper going on.

Think back to what you have already discovered so far in this study about thriving churches. Generosity permeates the congregations of these churches. It is true that congregations generally take on the personalities and the priorities of the pastor. So, apparently the pastor is doing a good job in this respect. We also learned that they are intentional in reaching out to the community. Again, that takes leadership on the part of the pastor. The research revealed that these churches are marked by vitality or, in other words, lots of passion and energy in their worship services. Once again, the influence of an effective leader is a critical dynamic.

The next discovery was that the members are empowered and equipped. That requires leadership also with the pastor taking time to invest in volunteers. We further observed that exceptional leadership is the hallmark of pastors leading these churches. So, if these pastors exercise excellent leadership, they must have it all together, right? The reality is there are no perfect churches, and there are no perfect pastors. You should be encouraged by this. Every leader has work to do, and the struggle to improve and to maximize effectiveness never ends, regardless of tenure, experience, or the state of the local church. Perhaps, that is why Paul reminded the church of Galatia, "Do not grow weary in well doing…" [Galatians 6:9] Ministry is frustrating, and pastors face challenges day in and day out. The challenges compete with priorities and, in turn, actions compete with ideas and vision.

Pastors often know what needs to be done but finding the time to do it is a common challenge. Why do pastors struggle to maintain priorities? Here are some reasons why pastors struggle with priorities. He is not just a pastor. The pastor is also ordinarily a husband, a father, and a member of the community. About half are bi-vocational and have responsibilities related to employment or their own business. His ministry, though it takes much time, is not a 24/7 proposition. He must first attend to his own family and to the needs of his home. The reality is that his own family is superior in importance and priority to the needs of his church. If he loses his family relationships, he will likely lose his ministry.

The demands of the pastor are multifaceted: evangelism, discipleship, fellowship, worship, ministry, and prayer. Those are the elements of ministry mentioned in Acts 2:42-47. That is the beginning of his responsibilities and not the total summary. How about the needs of the congregation? How about the administrative tasks of leading a congregation?

What about committees, teams, or church groups that the pastor must be engaged with? What about hospitals, illnesses, and visitation? What about funerals and weddings? What about counseling? The demands are multifaceted and often misunderstood and underappreciated by the members who know he preaches on Sunday and wonder what he does the rest of the week. The reality of so many facets to effective ministry make applying priorities quite a challenge.

Crises, problems and obstacles don't follow schedules. While a pastor may know what he intends to do on a particular day or in a particular week, he also understands that he deals with people and people have problems. When you minister to a group of 25, 125, 250, or 1,000 plus, someone in the congregation is in crisis at all points during each week. Often the pastor is expected to be engaged on some level, whether through prayer, encouragement, counsel, or hands-on assistance with the problems that arise. A pastor is perpetually responding, whether to some counseling issues, some crisis, a death in a family, or marital problems, in addition to sermon preparation and day-to-day pastoral leadership obligations. The pastor is subject to be confronted with multiple congregational issues at any time, day, or night.

Every pastor deals with squeaky wheels. You know what the squeaky wheel is. People say, "The squeaky wheel gets the grease." Pastors understand that many people cry for their attention. Many, if not most of the requests for the pastor's attention are legitimate. Even though some are not, the pastor is often expected to respond.

People are naturally inclined to gravitate to easier tasks. The pastor is not exempt from this. Given the choice of doing something that is very difficult or doing something that is relatively easy, human nature leads a person toward the easier task. The fact that all people are subject to their own human nature makes it difficult and challenging for anyone to maintain priorities.

Here's what you need to understand about pastors wrestling with priorities. This problem is not a detriment for those who wrestle with priorities, but rather with those who do not wrestle with them. The reality is that some pastors don't wrestle with priorities. They may not even know what the priorities are, or they just don't give intentional attention to them.

Be encouraged by this if you serve as a pastor, because if you are struggling, you are in good company. Even the pastor of the best church struggles. Understand that pastors from thriving churches struggle with priorities as they wrestle, with addressing and attacking the challenges they face.

As you wrestle with your priorities, here are four points of application:

Don't give up on what is important. For example, in Ephesians 4:12 the pastor is instructed to "equip the saints for the work of the ministry." It is not a suggestion given to those who may have the time. It is an actual assignment for the pastor. As important as preaching or a task, such as a hospital visitation, may be, Scripture reminds the pastor to equip his members to "do the work of the ministry." That would be easy if everyone would gladly respond. How often have you known a pastor that failed to provide any type of training for his members because "they would not respond?" You should not base your commitment to equipping other leaders by their response to your invitation, but, instead, on the biblical mandate and responsibility found in God's word. You do it, and, if you struggle, you find a way. That is what leaders do. You don't give up on what is important.

You must give attention to time management. Wrestling with priorities often comes down to this particular task or skill. You may or may not have administrative gifts as a pastor, but it is critical to your effectiveness to attend to several issues. This includes calendaring, task list management, prioritizing, drawing boundaries, and determining some core values that drive how you will and will not spend your time. If you do not determine how you are going to spend your time, others will determine it for you. You must be attentive to the way you manage your time.

Schedule those things that are most important. It is great to be spontaneous, and every pastor would do well to do so. However, since ministry is multifaceted and you will struggle with priorities, you should place on your calendar those things that are important. Here is an example, If I (Steve) only wrote when I felt like it, you would not be reading this. I learned a long time ago that I have to schedule days or portions of days to invest in research and writing. It is not an easy task. I would tend to gravitate to the easier tasks instead of writing. I schedule it, because it is important. I literally make an appointment for writing, such as I have today, so that the job will get done. It is a priority, so that I can maximize my influence.

Compare your schedule to your priorities. This particular task is a bit tedious but very revealing. First, what are your priorities? You can have more than one, but if you have 37, then you really don't have any. What are your top four, five, or maybe six priorities? Make a list. In this regard we are talking about priorities related to in your ministry. Family and personal health have precedence, but your ministry, what are your priorities? Next, take a couple of weeks and while doing your work, keep a log of how you are spending your time. You need not track your activities minute by minute but in 15-30-minute blocks. At the conclusion of the allotted time, go back and see what percentage of time you are spending on your priorities. You may realize you are spending more time on things less important. This is one of the ways that you can wrestle with your priorities. It is tedious; it is difficult; it is challenging; and you must wrestle with priorities, because the cultural landscape is shifting. You will need to give more and more time to those things that make the greatest difference, if you desire to be effective. Therefore, wrestle with priorities.

CHAPTER SEVEN
APPROACHABILITY

The book *Why They Stay?* addresses the issues that keep children and teens connected to church into their adult lives. It is based on a national research project of young adults ages 26-39 who grew up attending church. While much has been written about why young people are leaving the church, this book took a different approach. The research examined those who grew up in church and stayed faithful into their adult lives. The results of the research were groundbreaking. Fifteen major issues were uncovered that affect the likelihood that those that grew up in church will be there when they are adults.

One of the fifteen major issues in particular was unique to the research and should inspire you as a pastor. The research revealed that those who grew up in church and remained into their adult lives "loved their pastor when they were growing up." It makes sense when you think about it. A child who does not like his or her pastor when he or she is growing up will tend to attribute the ill feelings not just to their own pastor, but to pastors in general. If a child has difficulty connecting with his or her own pastor, quite frankly, it becomes more challenging for him or her to develop a love for God. The research highlighted the value and importance of the personal relationship between pastors and teens that affect them literally into their adult lives.

While conducting this research on vibrant churches in changing communities, we found a similar attribute that is of great interest and applies universally. The new research clearly revealed that pastors in these thriving churches are very approachable and accessible. These pastors build genuine relationships with the members of the congregation and the community. The pastors leading these churches are personable and they personally connect with the members. The average pastor ranked relationship building one of the top three priorities in the ministry, those that led vibrant churches actually spent more time building the relationships. The difference was significant. On average vibrant church pastors spend nearly 30 minutes a week more building relationships than other pastors.

Historically, there have been several philosophies driving the way that pastors relate to their members. Some seminary classes taught in years past that a pastor should be cautioned not to get too close to members. There is a risk as well as a reward when a pastor connects closely with the members. Just as a parent must be cautious in not choosing a favorite between children it was proposed that pastors should be cautious about choosing favorites among their members. Sometimes pastors have to make difficult leadership decisions. Those decisions might be compromised if they are too close to the members. Therefore, the prevailing philosophy for many years was that a pastor should not allow himself to get too attached. Here are some examples of approaches to pastor-church member relations. One would be the "CEO (Chief Executive Officer) approach." This is the method where a pastor sees himself as the primary and key leader, setting himself above the average member. You would be hard pressed to get an appointment with this pastor unless there is some extreme emergency or you are in some type of formal leadership or ministry setting. He approaches his ministry like a business, leading from the pulpit on Sunday but from behind the scenes during the week.

A second method would be the "Doctor approach." While no one begrudges a pastor for excelling in his academic pursuits, it can be detrimental to have an approach that comes across as audacious to the members. While there is nothing wrong with having a title such as "Doctor," the title should not be a barrier to the relationship between a pastor and his members.

The third method is that of the "preacher approach." Notice in some churches the pastor is called "The Preacher." While he is a preacher, that can be a very impersonal adjective. The emphasis is on what he does from the pulpit. You should note that for children and teens in particular, the closer the personal relationship with the pastor, the more likely they are to listen to the sermon.

Number four is the "closed gate approach." While the pastor may be personable in the pulpit as well as before or after Sunday morning services, he will rarely allow anyone to have an appointment or audience with him Monday through Saturday. Some pastors do not even live in the community where their church is located and interaction with members is limited while interaction with the community is virtually non-existent. Surprisingly, some members in churches like this wonder why the church is struggling.

Perhaps there is some element in each of these approaches that has merit. The point is not that pastors need no boundaries. They certainly do and should not allow themselves to be abused by overly needy members. Every pastor has experienced a member who lives with perpetual problems and demands way too much of his time and occasionally encounters a needy member who simply seeks lots of attention even in the best of times.

Though the applications of this point may sound obvious to some, the results of our comparative survey of several hundred other churches prove that they are not. Clearly some pastors are more effective at personally connecting with members than others. Be reminded again the research revealed that the pastors in thriving churches were more personable and connected to their members. The pulpit ministry can certainly be an asset, but it only goes so far. You can help people get to know you in the pulpit by being transparent and telling stories about yourself and your own personal journey. Certainly a few minutes invested before and after the service can also make some difference. How is your relationship with your members, not as a body, but as many individuals? What kinds of actions can you take that can help? Here are some ideas.

First, interact broadly with church members and guests. Take advantage of the times when members already gather such as Sunday mornings and during personal gatherings. John Maxwell (www.johnmaxwell.com/blog/managing-the-disciplines-of-relationship-building) refers to this as approach as "walking slowly through the crowd." It means on Sundays that you seek to arrive early and be accessible to your members. It means walking among Bible study groups, walking through the hallways or the auditorium prior to the service and personally interacting with as many people as possible. That approach would be in contrast to the pastor who is hidden away in an office waiting to make an appearance once the service begins. As you interact with members and guests alike you show personal interest in them. While you may only spend 30-45 seconds or a few minutes, these brief encounters can go a long way towards helping you to come across as personable to your members, helping them feel they have a relationship with you. Be sure to interact broadly with your members.

Second, make yourself accessible to as many of your members as possible. This will be different if you lead a smaller congregation compared to a larger church. The way you would make yourself available to a congregation of 75 and to a congregation of 2,500 is quite different. However, you do need to determine how you will approach this based on the size of the congregation that God has given you to lead. The key is to give your members a sense that you are accessible. How can a member have a conversation with you, whether through email or in person? Are you available to respond to the need or concern of a member? Apart from crisis moments some ways you can connect and be more accessible might include attending selected church events, participating in community events, lunch or dinner engagements with key leaders or couples, leading a small group Bible study, pastor receptions following services, coaching a community team, participating in recreational activities with members or going on retreats with members. In addition, being available during crisis moments, when possible, can also deepen relationships in a powerful way.

Third, invest in key relationships. It is important that you spend extended time with as many people as possible. Every leader has limited time and emotional resources. You cannot deeply connect with hundreds or thousands of people, but it can be accomplished with dozens of people. No matter what size congregation you lead it is crucial that you spend time investing in key relationships. Bear in mind that for pastors in thriving churches this is a mark of their leadership. They come across as approachable to their members and they build genuine relationships. One other note--it has been said that change moves at the speed of trust. What is it that compels people to trust their pastor? The bottom line is this: you trust people that you care for and that you love. Therefore, the more people that care for you and love you, the more they will trust you and ultimately love and respect you. That is important as you seek to lead your congregation toward needed changes. Because, if indeed change moves at the speed of trust, that trust is ultimately built on the strength of your relationship with the members and key leaders. Therefore, be purposeful in being personable and it will enhance your leadership.

CHAPTER EIGHT
KINDNESS AND COMPASSION

Have you ever used the expression, "Let's Go to Church?" You can say it with no ill intent, but the reality is that the church is not a building or a geographical location.

The church is not a place that someone goes to, if you consider it from a purely biblical perspective. The church is a group of people dispersed throughout the community. While the church often gathers at a central location, it is not the building. For many congregations the primary focus is what happens in a building that we are prone to inadvertently refer to as "the church."

For the congregations that are thriving in a changing culture, the church is not simply a philosophical concept. Members literally penetrate and infiltrate their communities, making a tangible difference off the property, as well as on the campus. They possess a kindness and compassion that is tangibly expressed, as needs in the community are met. You may recall earlier how we discussed churches that thrive in a changing culture are prone to provide strong, benevolent ministries. This may have been a mild surprise. Providing benevolent ministries is challenging work, because it brings small and sometimes no return, even though these churches invest themselves in the lives of others.

Four things surfaced in the study of churches that thrive in a changing culture. First, these congregations have an outward focus. There is an exercise that I often do when equipping leaders of Bible study groups. I will bring up a group of four to six people, and ask them to join hands, and form a circle. You can envision what takes place. The people walk forward and join hands and forming a circle looking at each other in the circle. I have done this over a hundred times and received the same response every time. They never join hands looking away from each other; they always look inward. I follow up by asking those that have joined hands and formed the circle to turn and face outward. As they join hands once again, I share some observations. As they face outward, they are still connected, just like they were when they faced inward. Not only are they still connected, but they are as close to one another as they were before. There is more than one way to join hands and form a circle. You can join hands and face inward, or you can join hands and focus outward.

Are you acquainted with the text in Luke 5 about the parable of the lost sheep? You will recall how there were 100 sheep, until one strayed away. The shepherd, according to the text, left the 99 and went after the one that was lost. That is a great biblical example of outward focus. It does not mean that you cannot stay connected, or that you cannot remain close. As a matter of fact, those that join hands and form a circle facing outward are still there for each other, but the focus has changed. This is the model that we found in churches that thrive in the midst of a changing culture. They are close, and they are connected; but the focus is not primarily on one another. The focus, instead, is on the community.

Focusing on the community does not take away from their love for one another. Instead, it makes a difference not only in the community, but in their own lives as well.

The thriving churches sacrificially give to missions and ministries beyond the four walls. These churches give well above average to missions in their community, in their state, nationally and internationally. They designate annual, budgeted funds and give sacrificially to meet the needs of those who are not members. That same spirit was expressed earlier as we discussed the benevolent ministries. These churches willingly expend resources on non-members who are in need and may never attend services in that church. They willingly send money forth to others who are making a difference in lives of people around the world, and the amount they give is not small. They give sacrificially. They give up things they could do for themselves, for their own congregation, or for their own facilities, in order to touch the lives of people who will never walk on the property. By doing this they believe that doors will be opened to the gospel, and that people they never meet will come to faith in Christ.

Thriving churches are visible in the community. Not everything in these churches takes place in their facilities. These congregations do things on the property and invite the community; but they are also prone to do things in the community. They take the approach that if the fish will not come to the boat, you take the boat to where the fish are. While they are purposeful in conducting ministry off-site, they also open their facilities to the community as a method of ministry.

While you can understand that a church might have some gate or barrier to prevent large trucks from turning around in the parking lot so as to not damage the asphalt, these churches are more likely to risk the damage so as not to appear to be closed to the community. Their facilities and their property are open to community groups for recreational teams or for community meetings. Their recreational facilities are not simply clubs for members, but tools used for reaching out to the community. Perhaps you've heard it suggested that some churches could disappear, and the community would not even know they were gone. That is a good question to ask about your congregation. If your church literally disappeared, would your community even know that it had left? Would your church be missed by those who are not members? Thriving churches are actively involved in their community. That is how they are able to make such a difference. They make a difference in a changing culture, because they engage the culture.

Expanding a bit on the last point, thriving churches are purposeful in connecting with their community. They do things in the community by design. Do not miss the importance of this. As a matter of fact, this variable was the top-ranked variable in our study. There was no other variable showing more of a difference between the two groups. Vibrant churches conduct ministries and activities by connecting to the community, specifically with the unchurched, in mind. Georgia Baptists conducted a research project some years ago, studying the strongest, evangelistic churches in the state. One of the questions asked was, "What is your church doing that is effective in reaching people?" The purpose of the question was to discover one or two key strategies commonly found in churches that could be shared with others, so that they could likewise implement them in order to reach their communities. The interesting discovery was that more than 50 different ministry activities were reported by the churches, which were being utilized to reach people, in their communities. The research concluded it is not the *activity* that helps your church to reach people, it is the *strategy* behind the activity.

As an example, any church can have a softball team. One church can have a men's softball team that is used to do outreach, and another could have a men's softball team to minister to the members. One church can provide a Christian camp for teenagers or children to minister to their members, while another could use a similar camp to reach out to the community and the unchurched, as well as to minister to members. One church can hold a fish fry to enjoy fellowship among the members, while another can utilize a fish fry as an outreach activity for people who have never been to church. You can utilize almost any activity to minister to members; or to engage the community, and reach out to the lost. It is a choice. That choice is what sets the thriving churches apart. They take their activities into the community and they open up their property and facilities to the community. As they conduct ministry and activities, they do so with the community in mind. They do things for the community to meet needs, and that, in turn, opens up the door for the gospel to be shared with even more people; and the impact is notable. Thriving churches make a difference even in the midst of a changing culture. They are living expressions of kindness and compassion to their communities.

CHAPTER NINE
EXTERNAL CONNECTIONS

Have you noticed how competitive churches can be between one another? The reality is churches cannot exist without members. Without members there is no local church. The result is a temptation to compete for members who can sustain the local congregation or to reach new heights of growth. The competition may or may not be overt, may or may not be done with ill intent, and may or may not be done for the purpose of hurting anyone. In any case, an undercurrent of competition does exist.

The reality is that if everyone in the community showed up for services on a Sunday morning, there would not be enough room in existing churches to accommodate everyone. There is no need to compete for other church members when the greatest need is to reach those who are lost without Jesus Christ. Churches should always seek to have a Kingdom mindset. You will find that attitude prevailing among the churches that thrive in a changing culture.

They have relationships with other churches that may be a surprise to you. You might think churches thrive, because they do so well in competing for and winning members. Perhaps, the reason they are thriving is because they are skilled at winning members away from other churches. You would be correct if you assume that they tend to attract people, because they do many things well, but that is not their focus or intent. The study revealed that thriving churches do not focus on competing with other churches, but are surprisingly more inclined to cooperate with other churches. Within the top variables where a significant difference was measured, variables ranked number six, seven, and eight were all related to investing in relationships with other churches.

These churches are purposeful about having external connections with other congregations. Thriving churches tend to have strong relationships with other churches within their community and networks beyond. The pastors and leaders have a Kingdom mindset that takes the approach of investing in other churches in hopes of making them stronger. They identify and recognize their own strengths and while not perfect, desire to do what they can to help other congregations become healthier and stronger. In these churches, unity and cooperation are valued above competition.

How is it that a church can be strong, healthy, thriving, and perhaps growing without being competitive? The application given below will give you a sense of how they do it, and how you can make a difference not only in your own congregation and in your community, but in other congregations as well.

Understand what is unique about your congregation. There is also a second part to this point. Not only do you need to recognize what is unique about your congregation, but you need to understand what is unique about other congregations in your community. It is certainly easy to draw a conclusion about what makes your congregation stand apart. Are you willing to invest the time to discover what makes the other congregations unique? Perhaps, it is the culture of the church that makes it different from the other churches in the community. It could be the size of the church. Certainly, different size congregations offer different advantages and disadvantages to church prospects. Perhaps, it is the style of music that makes one church stand out from another. It could be the polity, the way the church is organized, or the way it conducts its business. Maybe the differences are in programs offered, what is offered for senior adults, children, young adults, married couples, or college students. In addition, if different denominations are involved, the differences could relate to the doctrines that the churches tend to emphasize. Sometimes, preaching styles are different even when doctrine is the same. Why is it important for you to understand the uniqueness of the other congregations? What if, instead of competing, we understood what our strengths are, as well as the strengths of the other congregations, and championed one another instead of complaining or competing? For example, what if someone comes to your church, and they do not prefer the style of music? The first hope is that they would overlook that and consider other positive qualities possessed by your church. But if it matters greatly to them, perhaps you know of a church in your community that has a style of music that they would prefer. Perhaps, it is a church that is consistent with your doctrinal convictions but differs in their style. Why would you not refer them to that church?

Likewise, if that pastor understands what makes your church stand apart, he could recommend someone your way. What if pastors worked together? That is what leaders in thriving churches do.

They understand what is unique about them, as well as what is unique about the other churches in their community.

Get to know other pastors. Actually, point one and two can go in any order, and they do fit together. The best way to know what is unique about other congregations is to spend time with the pastors. Like-minded pastors may not line up with you on every finer point of theology and doctrine, but when you can agree on the central doctrine of Jesus as the only begotten Son of God; born of a virgin; lived a sinless life; died an atoning death for the sins of man; physically resurrected from the dead; the only way of salvation; returning for His Bride, the church, at His second coming—then you can work together. Most Christian churches and all evangelical congregations fall within this doctrinal framework. In addition, most towns have other Southern Baptist churches and the cooperation there is critical, not only to your witness but to the effectiveness of the denomination.

It is important in a Kingdom mindset not only that pastors in your community connect, but that you pray for one another, encourage one another, and work together with a unified purpose. Healthy inter-church relationships will help you not only discover the uniqueness of the other congregations, but also serve as points of prayer support, accountability, encouragement, and personal growth. How do you spend time and get to know the pastors in your community? As a matter of fact, do you know the pastors in your community, particularly those of other evangelical congregations? Begin, first, with other Southern Baptist churches, but then get to know the other churches that would share core doctrines and values with us as Southern Baptists.

Consider what you can do in partnership with other congregations? How might it affect your community if they were to see churches working together, instead of working against one another? What if they see a unity among us? Do you recall in the seventeenth chapter of the gospel of John how Jesus prayed that His followers would be one, and that the body of believers would exercise unity? You may recall how Jesus said that people would know Christians by their love for one another. Is it not important that your community members, those that do not know Christ, see churches loving one another and working together instead of competing? The reality is that churches can reach more together than they can reach on their own.

Thriving churches seek to lift up struggling churches. What is your church currently doing tangibly, not philosophically, to help congregations that are struggling? Here is an example, I (Steve) was recently speaking with a group of student pastors and asked them if they knew how many Georgia churches had a full-time or part-time vocational student pastor? Do you know the answer? There are approximately 3,600 Southern Baptist churches in Georgia. How many do you suppose have a full-time or part-time vocational student pastor? The answer is around 400. What about the other 3,200? While we know that volunteers can do an excellent job with students in the community, they would certainly benefit from someone who has full time to invest in the needs and methods of reaching young people in the community. Does your church have a full-time vocational student pastor? Would you consider granting that student pastor one, two, or three days each month, not to invest in the students in your church or not to invest in the members of your church, but to invest in other churches in your community that do not have a vocational student pastor? That is just one simple example of a church having a Kingdom mindset, knowing the strengths they have, and considering how they might help other churches that are struggling.

The aim, in this case, is not to send your student pastor to another church to get their students to come to your church. The design is to send this person a day or two each month to another church, at no expense to them, in order to corporately reach more together. What is it that you are doing well? When is the last time you released members or staff to assist a struggling congregation? Consider this principle from the other perspective also. Perhaps, there is some area where your church is struggling. Do not be too prideful to allow pastors, members, and leaders to come and assist you in strengthening that area where your church needs improvement. If your church needs help, you are in good company. Most do, but far too many fail to open themselves to the assistance of others from outside the immediate congregation. The relationship that your church has with other congregations is important, and it is interesting to discover that thriving churches in the midst of a changing culture actually are intentional about building relationships with other churches. Go and do thou likewise!

THE RESEARCH PROCESS

A multifaceted qualitative study was preformed that identified several themes related to new church health metrics. First, interviews, focus groups, and surveys were conducted to determine if a set of themes were prevalent in current church leader perspectives. During the interviews and focus group discussions, a biblical model was identified and adopted to frame the information found in a literature review phase and the interview phase of the study. The biblical framework focused on the Great Commission and the Great Commandment passages in the New Testament. Leaders' opinions were drawn from a variety of settings and locations around the state of Georgia, including small rural settings, suburban settings, new church plants, and church leaders from a variety of church leadership structures. In addition, associational missionary leaders from three distinct regions of the state—northeast, south, and central Georgia—were polled and interviewed. In addition, state missionaries of the Georgia Baptist Mission Board were interviewed. The information was consolidated into a matrix identified as hypothesized core essentials for church health.

A comprehensive study of the recent church health/growth literature was conducted, producing a similar matrix of hypothesized core essentials. The first two phases informed the development of a questionnaire. The third phase of the study included the deployment of the questionnaire to pastors in Georgia. The questionnaire was specifically used to measure significant differences in the opinions, motivations, and attitudes of pastors of healthier churches in Georgia. The standard for health was established by the staff of the Georgia Baptist Mission Board and focused on the core essentials identified in phases one and two of the study. Churches were placed into two categories based upon the standard. An email deployment of the questionnaire was used for convenience. In the study, 1,832 pastor emails were identified and used. Of these, 72 churches were labeled as "group A," as they scored in the 98th percentile of all churches using a formula comprised of available statistics and qualitative evaluations from Georgia Baptist Mission Board staff. A total of 1,762 churches were identified as "Group B." Questionnaires were sent to 1,834 pastors in Georgia through the Survey Monkey online delivery system. Of these, 417 participated in the study: 37 "A" pastors participated and 370 "B" pastors participated.

The questionnaire focused on five core attitudes, opinions, and motivations related to the findings of the first two phases of the study. A series of two sample t-tests were applied to the results to determine if a significant difference existed between groups. The results showed differences in the attitudes, opinions, and motivations of the "A" church pastors and the "B" church pastors.

Next, the questionnaire was renamed "Pastor Perspective Survey" and was deployed as part of the Annual Church Report process for 2016. Pastors were asked to share, using the same survey. Of these pastors, 720 completed the survey, and the results were added to the original study; and identical tests were run to confirm the data. A total of 1,127 total surveys were completed. Findings were confirmed using a series of two sample t-tests to determine if significant differences existed between perceptions of pastors in each of the two groups. Decisions were made whether to reject each of the null hypothesis based on each of its corresponding test. Additional analysis was completed using the ranked scores, ranked averages, and ranked percentages of the priorities and time spent preforming certain pastoral tasks.

ABOUT THE AUTHORS

Dr. Steve Parr serves the Georgia Baptist Mission Board as the Vice President of Staff Coordination and Development. In 30 years of ministry he has assisted hundreds of churches in strengthening their ministries, by motivating and training leaders through seminars, conferences, preaching, and personal consultations. Steve has a Masters of Divinity Degree in Christian Education from New Orleans Baptist Theological Seminary and a Doctor of Ministry degree in Church Growth and Evangelism from The Southern Baptist Theological Seminary. He was featured on the twentieth anniversary of the Billy Graham School of Evangelism of Southern Seminary as one of 20 alumni making a Great Commission impact around the world in 2014.

Steve is a best-selling author of six books, including *Why They Stay, The Coffee Shop That Changed a Church, Sunday School That Really Excels, Sunday School That Really Responds, Sunday School That Really Works,* and *Evangelistic Effectiveness*; *Differences in Mindsets and Methods.* Steve is married to Carolyn and has three adult children, Leah, Lauren, and Larissa; and two sons-in-law and two grandchildren. Follow him on Twitter @steverparr and check out his resources and blog on *Maximized Leadership* at www.steveparr.net.

Dr. Tom Crites has served and studied churches for more than 25 years. He has the unique opportunity to study church health through his work as the Research Specialist of the Georgia Baptist Mission Board. He remains on the cutting edge of recent developments in church life through his teaching and mentorship at Liberty University. He has his Masters of Divinity degree and Doctorate of Education degree in Educational Leadership from Southeastern Baptist Theological Seminary. He has presented research in many scholarly settings and has had his books and research articles read by thousands of ministers across the country. Tom co-wrote *Why They Stay & Evangelistic Effectiveness; Differences in Mindsets and Methods with Steve.*

Tom is married to Cyndy and has two adult children, Kaylynn and Brice. Find him on Linked In, Twitter @ltomcrites, and Facebook.

NOTES

1 Steve Parr & Tom Crites, *Why They Stay: Helping Parents and Church Leaders Make Investments That Keep Children and Teens Connected to the Church for a Lifetime* (Bloomington, IN: Westbow Press, 2015). Especially look at chapter two to get an understanding of current reality.

2 John Dickerson, *The Great Evangelical Recession: 6 Factors That Will Crash the American Church... and How to Prepare* (Ada, MI: Baker Books, 2013). Contains a sobering account of the possible future of the church and Calvin Miller, *The Vanishing Evangelical: Saving the Church from its Own Success by Restoring What Really Matters* (Ada, MI: Baker Books, 2013). In his last book, Miller passionately puts his finger in the face of the problem with the American church.

3 Thom Rainer, *The Bridger Generation: America's Second Largest Generation, What They Believe and How to Reach Them* (Nashville, TN: Broadman & Holman, 2006), 169. Offers glimmers of hope.

4 Christian Smith, *Soul Searching: The Religious and Spiritual Lives of American Teenagers* (New York: Oxford University Press, Inc., 2005), 170.

5 Gabe Lyons & David Kinnaman, *Unchristian: What a New Generation Really Thinks about Christianity and Why It Matters* (Grand Rapids, MI: Baker Books, 2007).

6 David Kim, *20 and Something: Have the Time of Your Life (and Figure It Out Too)* (Grand Rapids, MI: Zondervan, 2013), 84.

7 Calvin Miller, *The Vanishing Evangelical.* Look particularly at the first two chapters.

8 Bulley, G. (2016) *Ministry in the New Reality.* [white paper], 14.

9 Ibid

10 Ibid, 15.

11 Crites, T (2015). Georgia statistical summary. *Georgia Baptist Convention Annual Minutes.*

12 U.S. Census Bureau, (2015). Current population survey, annual social and economic supplements. "Population and Per Capita Money Income, All Races: 1967 to 2015." Retrieved from www2.census.gov/programs-surveys/cps/techdocs.cpsmar16.pdf.

13 The calculation was based on the Department of Labor; Bureau of Labor Statistics' CPI Inflation Calculator Retrieved from http://www.bls.gov/data/inflation_calculator.htm. The CPI inflation calculator uses the average Consumer Price Index for a given calendar year. This data represents changes in prices of all goods and services purchased for consumption by urban households. This index value has been calculated every year since 1913. For the current year, the latest monthly index value is used.

14 Whitney, D. (1991). *Spiritual Disciplines for the Christian Life,* 140. Colorado Springs, CO: NavPress Publishing Group.15Ed Stetzer, Turn Around Churches (Nashville, TN: Broadman & Holman Publishing, 2003).

15 Bulley, G. (2016) *Ministry in the New Reality.* [white paper], 27-28.

16 Pew Research Center. (2012). *Nones on the rise: One-in-five adults have no religious affiliation.* Retrieved from http://www.pewforum.org/2012/10/09/nones-on-the-rise-religion/#what-keeps-people-out-of-the-pews

17 David Olsen, *The American Church in Crisis* (Grand Rapids, MI: Zondervan, 2008).

18 P. Bush, I*n Dying We Are Born: The Challenge and The Hope for Congregations* (Herndon, VA: Alban Institute, 2008).

19 Ed Stetzer, *Turn Around Churches* (Nashville, TN: Broadman & Holman Publishing, 2003).

20 M. McCormack, *"Study Updates Stats on Health of Southern Baptist Churches."* Retrieved from http://www.bpnews.net/BPnewsasp?ID=19542.

21 Findley Edge, *A Quest for Vitality in Religion* (Nashville, TN: Broadman & Holman Publishing, 1963).

22 Ibid page 9. See his chapter on authentic faith especially the section subtitled "Elements Involved in Authentic Faith." pages 165 – 178.

23 Henry Blackaby, Richard Blackaby & Claude King, *Experiencing God: Knowing and Doing the Will of God* (Nashville, TN: B&H Publishing Group, 2008) 116.

24 1 Corinthians 12.

25 Robby Gallaty is the senior pastor of Long Hollow Baptist Church in Hendersonville, TN. He is the author of *Growing Up: How to Be a Disciple Who Makes Disciples, Unashamed: Taking a Radical Stand for Christ and Creating an Atmosphere to HEAR God Speak.* Lots of great resources are on his website: http://replicate.org

26 Thom Rainer & Eric Geiger, *Simple Church* (Nashville: B & H Publishing, 1996), 113.

27 Bill Hull, *Disciple-Making Pastor: Leading Others on the Journey of Faith* (Ada, MI: Baker Books, 2007), 54.

28 Brad J. Waggoner, *The Shape of Faith to Come* (Nashville, TN: B & H Publishing Group, 2008), 12.

29 Robby Gallaty gave us permission to reprint portions of his article from LifeWay Leadership, http://www.lifeway.com/leadership/2014/06/17/creating-a-discipleship-culture-in-the-local-church/

30 Steve Parr & Tom Crites, *Why They Stay: Helping Parents and Church Leaders Make Investments That Keep Children and Teens Connected to the Church for a Lifetime* (Bloomington, IN: Westbow Press, 2015).

31 John Maxwell. (2013). *Managing the disciplines of relationship-building.* Retrieved from http://www.johnmaxwell.com/blog/managing-the-disciplines-of-relationship-building

www.ingramcontent.com/pod-product-compliance
Lightning Source LLC
Chambersburg PA
CBHW071529080526
44588CB00011B/1615